The TIME *trekkers* visit the MIDDLE AGES

KATE NEEDHAM

COPPER BEECH BOOKS
BROOKFIELD, CONNECTICUT

Designed and produced by
Aladdin Books Ltd
28 Percy Street
London W1P 0LD

First published in the United States in 1996 by
Copper Beech Books, an imprint of
The Millbrook Press
2 Old New Milford Road
Brookfield, Connecticut 06804

Editor
Jim Pipe
Designed by
David West Children's Books
Designer
Simon Morse
Illustrated by
Sheena Vickers
Additional illustrations by
Ian Thompson, David Burroughs

Printed in Belgium

Library of Congress Cataloging-in-Publication Data
Needham, Kate.
The Middle Ages / by Kate Needham: illustrated by Sheena Vickers and Dave Burroughs. p. cm. -- (The time trekkers visit the--) Summary: includes information on how to become a knight, how castles are built, the plague of the Black Death, medieval feasts, and dungeons.
ISBN 0-7613-0481-9 (lib. bdg.). -- ISBN 0-7613-0482-7 (pbk.) 1. Middle Ages--Juvenile literature. 2. Civilization, Medieval--Juvenile literature. [1. Middle Ages. 2. Civilization, Medieval.] I. Vickers, Sheena, ill. II Burroughs, Dave. 1952- ill. III. Title. IV. Series.
CB351.N44 1996 95-39832
940.1--dc20 CIP AC

CONTENTS

Introduction

The Time trekkers are Lucy, Jools, Eddie, and Sam. Using the time machine invented by Lucy's eccentric grandfather, they travel through time and space on amazing voyages of discovery. Their gizmos are always ready to answer any questions!

But before we follow their journey back to the colorful world of the Middle Ages, let's meet the four adventurers...

The Time Trekkers

Lucy – As she is the oldest of the four travelers, Lucy gets a bit bossy at times. But when the going gets tough, the others rely on her to save the day.

Jools – is always in a rush to get somewhere, but when he stops he usually gets caught up in the local wildlife. His pet frog, Kevin, isn't always easy to find.

Eddie – With his knowledge of history, it's Eddie's job to set the controls on the time machine. The only problem is the fact that he's a bit of a dreamer!

Sam – When the time machine starts playing up, call Sam, the research scientist. She's a whiz with all kinds of gadgets, but she gets so wrapped up in her walkman that she often doesn't notice the danger around her!

The Gizmo

To use this book, simply read the Time trekkers' question bubbles, then look to the gizmo for the answer! There are three subject buttons:

- *Science (Orange)*
- *Places and People (Purple)*
- *History and Arts (Red)*

And two extra special buttons:

- *X ray (Yellow)*
- *Translator (Blue)*

Subject logo
ATTACKING A CASTLE
There are several ways to get past the castle walls. Attackers can:
1 use ladders, but defenders can easily push them away;
2 fill in the ditch and roll up a siege tower;
3 batter down the door;
4 dig a tunnel under a wall and then light a fire to make the wall collapse (below).
Gizmo's answer
Control panels

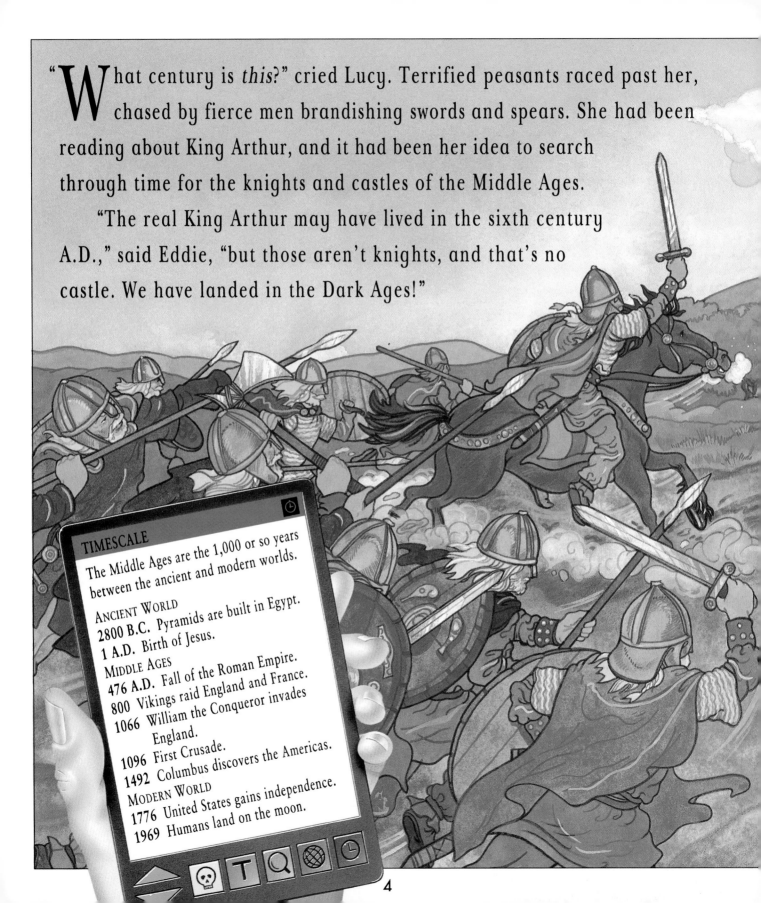

"What century is *this*?" cried Lucy. Terrified peasants raced past her, chased by fierce men brandishing swords and spears. She had been reading about King Arthur, and it had been her idea to search through time for the knights and castles of the Middle Ages.

"The real King Arthur may have lived in the sixth century A.D.," said Eddie, "but those aren't knights, and that's no castle. We have landed in the Dark Ages!"

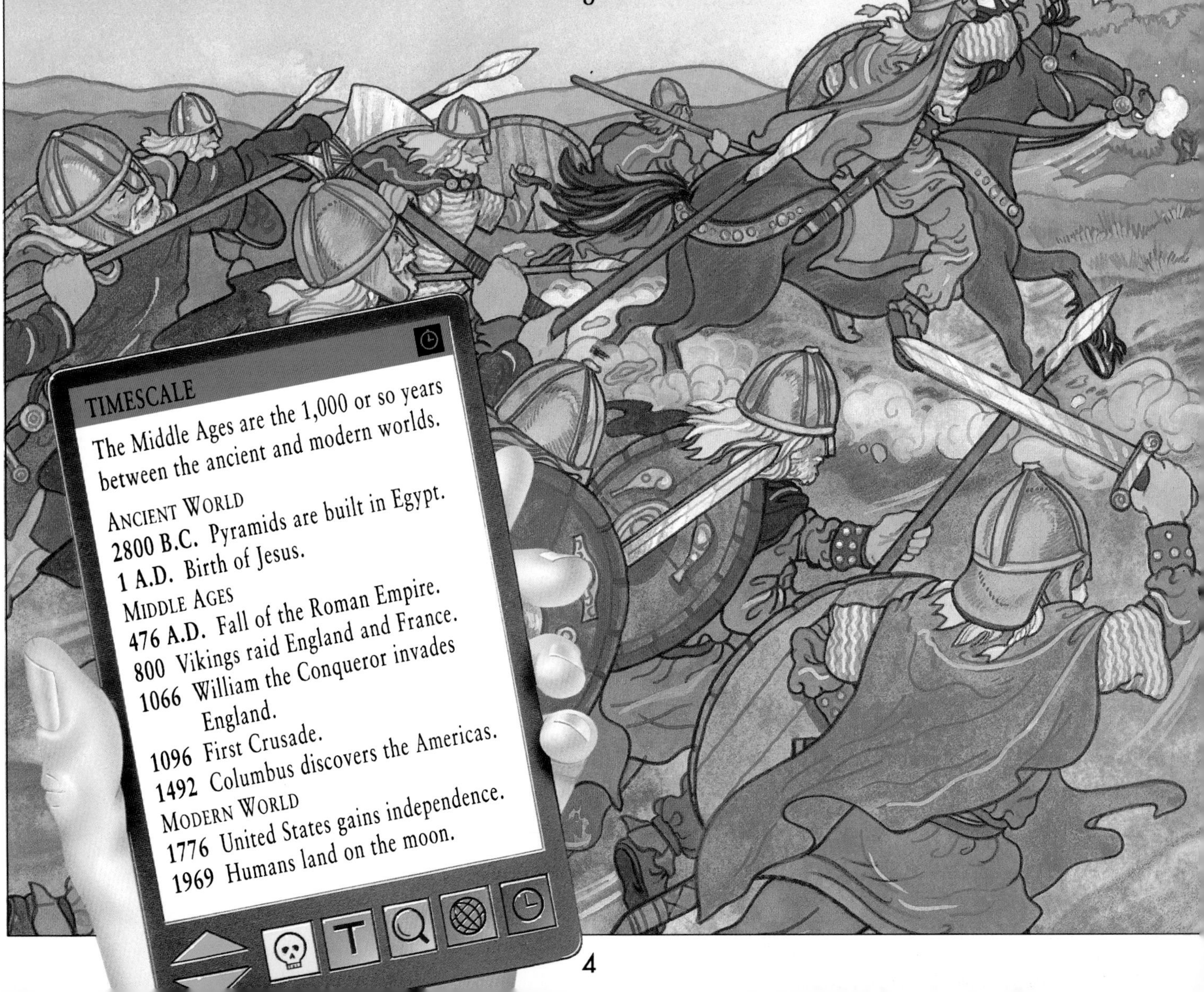

TIMESCALE
The Middle Ages are the 1,000 or so years between the ancient and modern worlds.
ANCIENT WORLD
2800 B.C. Pyramids are built in Egypt.
1 A.D. Birth of Jesus.
MIDDLE AGES
476 A.D. Fall of the Roman Empire.
800 Vikings raid England and France.
1066 William the Conqueror invades England.
1096 First Crusade.
1492 Columbus discovers the Americas.
MODERN WORLD
1776 United States gains independence.
1969 Humans land on the moon.
T

No one wanted to hang around, so Eddie reset the controls. "*Plus 750* should do it," he muttered as they traveled forward through time.

What are the Middle Ages in the middle of?
What's going on?

THE DARK AGES

Few books survive from this time, so we're not exactly sure! We do know that German tribes are invading Europe, destroying the town life and trade of the old Roman Empire.

Because of the constant wars and violence, this first part of the Middle Ages is called the Dark Ages. Only when a Germanic king, Charlemagne (*above*), conquers much of Europe, will some sort of order be created. He will be made Holy Roman Emperor by the Pope in 800 AD.

This time, the Time trekkers stepped out into a busy market square. A large crowd had gathered around a man who was shouting and ringing a bell. When they saw the four children, they all turned to stare. "Maybe it's our clothes," said Jools. "Everyone's wearing tunics and tights!"

Lucy, however, wasn't paying any attention. She had spotted the castle and was wondering where the knights were. "Look," shouted Sam, "everyone's headed toward the castle. Let's see what's going on!"

TOWN CRIER

The man ringing the bell is a town crier, whose job is to announce any news. He rings the bell to get people's attention.

This announcement is about a joust which is about to take place in the meadow below the castle.

You can't understand him, Jools, because he is speaking a mixture of Latin and French. During the Middle Ages, people in different parts of Europe gradually developed their own languages, based on Latin.

LIMITS OF TRAVEL

They're staring because your clothes look odd next to theirs. Also, they have probably never seen anyone with dark skin. Most medieval people stayed in the same place all their lives, and little was known of the world outside Europe (*above*).

JOUSTING

Knights come from far and wide to test their skills in a joust, which is an organized fight.

They wear full armor, helmets, and spurs (*below*) to make their horses gallop faster. They sometimes add a ribbon given to them by their favorite lady (*above left*). Each knight tries to knock the other off his horse. Then the fight continues on foot.

The weapons are blunt, but there are still many injuries.

HERALDRY

A knight who is in armor is hard to recognize, so each noble family chooses an emblem which they paint onto the shield and a tunic worn over the armor.

The design, known as a coat of arms, makes it easier to tell who is who in battle.

When two nobles marry, their children usually take the emblems of both families.

The Time trekkers followed the crowd to the meadow. A trumpet sounded, and two knights thundered toward each other. There was a clash of metal and the black knight was flung to the ground. Nearby, a boy cheered loudly. "Hi," he said, turning to Jools, "I'm Will, squire to Sir Humphrey, the red knight."

"Baron John and Lady Eleanor are having a feast tonight to celebrate the Crusade," he added. "Why don't you come?"

But Sam was so thrilled by this, she never noticed a pickpocket creeping up on her.

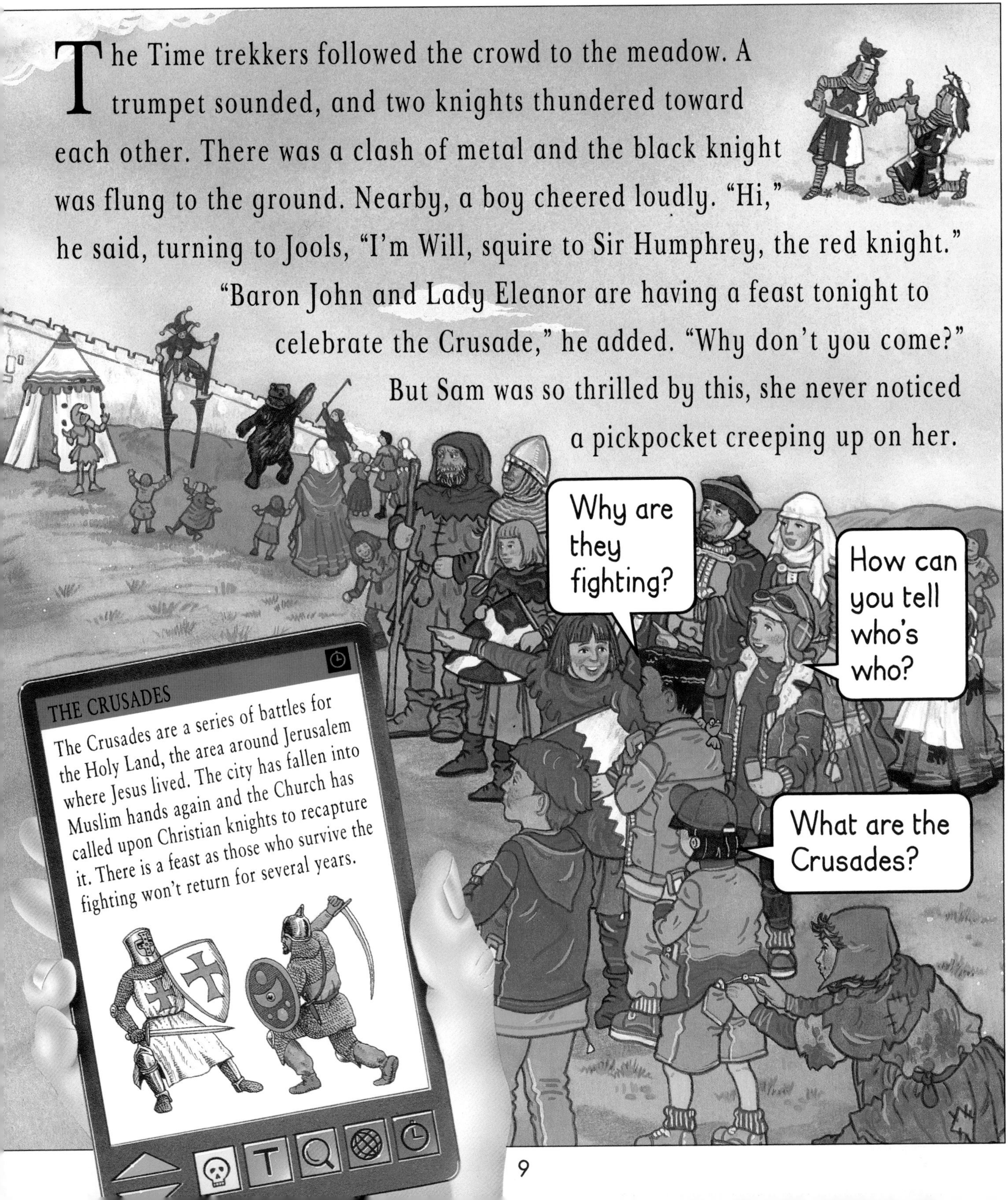

Why are they fighting?
How can you tell who's who?
What are the Crusades?

THE CRUSADES

The Crusades are a series of battles for the Holy Land, the area around Jerusalem where Jesus lived. The city has fallen into Muslim hands again and the Church has called upon Christian knights to recapture it. There is a feast as those who survive the fighting won't return for several years.

Why can't I eat with Lady Eleanor?
Has this bird been cooked?
THE FEUDAL SYSTEM
Because in the Middle Ages, Sam, society is divided into ranks by the feudal system. The King, at the top, gives land to men like Baron John, in return for his support. In turn, John gives land to his knights, for their help, and small plots to peasants, who also work on his land.
King
Baron
Knight
Merchant
Peasant

As it turned out, Will's invitation was to help serve the feast, not eat it! They certainly needed the extra hands. There were over 40 different dishes to carry out and endless jugs of ale to pour. People ate with their fingers and threw scraps on the floor. Only Baron John's table had plates. The rest used slices of stale bread.

Meanwhile, Sam was looking very worried. "I've lost the key to the time machine," she said, "so now we're trapped in the Middle Ages!"

FOOD

Yes, Jools, the birds are cooked. Their feathers were all stuck back on again afterward! The meat from the boar's head has been cooked and put back, too.

It has taken many staff several days to prepare it all. Outside the kitchens, beggars are waiting in line for scraps and the stale bread that was used as plates.

TOILETS

You might have second thoughts when you find out where the bathroom is, Eddie.

It's a small room in the side of the tower called a *garderobe* (*right*). There is no plumbing, just a hole in the wall.

As you can imagine, it smells pretty awful in the moat below!

They searched everywhere in vain for the key. "We can't go anywhere without it," moaned Jools. Luckily, Will had a word with Sir Humphrey, who persuaded Baron John and Lady Eleanor to let them stay at the castle. In exchange, they will have to train to become squires.

Sam thought this was great, but to her horror, she and Lucy were taken away to learn embroidery instead. "This is so unfair," Sam moaned as they watched from the balcony, "And look, the boys are completely useless anyway."

BECOMING A KNIGHT

Sorry Sam. Only boys from noble families can become knights. First, they are sent to serve a neighboring family as a page, to help out with tasks around the castle.

After a few years they'll become a squire. As a squire they look after their knight's horse and armor, and help him dress for battle. The King will decide when you are ready to be made a knight.

This squire is cleaning his knight's armor by rolling it in a barrel of sand.

WEAPONS
Mace
Axe
Longbow
Sword
Dagger
Arrows
What sort of weapons do we use?

Eddie and Jools proved so hopeless at fighting that they were sent to the local monastery for instruction from the monks.

It was a calm place after the noise and bustle of the castle. There were courtyards and chapels, dormitories for the monks, and even a hospital for the sick. And at last,

THE CHURCH
The Church in the Middle Ages is extremely rich and very powerful.
Everyone has to donate money, even the poor. The rich often give large sums. The Pope, who is head of the Church, has as much authority as the King.
This wealth is used to build many great cathedrals. They are made as tall as possible, to reflect the power of God.

Jools and Eddie were at the top of the class. They had both studied a little Latin, and the monks were amazed that they could read and write. Then... in walked the barber. Jools and Eddie took one look at the other monks' haircuts, and they were off. But not before the barber chopped a tuft of hair from Eddie's head!

What an enormous building!
How do they do it?
BUILDING
Cathedrals take about 100 years to build. Each stone has to be cut to size and hoisted into place.
Hundreds of skilled craftsmen work on details such as stone carvings or stained glass windows (*right*). Inside there will be ornate wooden paneling, tapestries, and paintings.
At the top of the tower you will see monsters' heads being carved into the stone used for gutters. Called *gargoyles*, these are supposed to scare off evil spirits.
T
[redacted]

Meanwhile, back at the castle, Lucy and Sam were very bored, so Lady Eleanor invited them on a shopping trip. It seemed better than sitting around all day, so off they went.

The town smelled rotten – garbage everywhere, with rats and flies swarming all over it. Lady

What is that awful smell?

DISEASE

Mind Your Head Lucy!

There are no sewers in town, so people throw their waste out into the streets. People are filthy, too. They rarely bathe (*above*).

It's not surprising that in a hundred years (1347), a terrible plague, known as the Black Death, will sweep through Europe, killing one in three people. It is spread by fleas (*above*) which live on rats.

Eleanor had given them each a small bunch of herbs to sniff, but it didn't help much. Then Lucy heard her discussing wedding plans loudly with a friend. As Lucy got closer, she couldn't believe her ears. The plans were for her and Sam! There was no time to lose – she had to find the boys and plan an escape.

What is that sign for?
TRADE SIGNS
Barber
Blacksmith
The signs advertise what each shop sells or makes. Most people can't read in the Middle Ages so shops have a picture instead of words.
Local goods, such as pottery, barrels, and belts are usually sold by the people who made them. Luxury items, like fine cloth, are imported from abroad.

"Nice haircut!" giggled Sam when she saw Eddie's bald patch. But she soon stopped laughing when he replied, "Thanks, I wanted to look good for your wedding." Luckily, Lucy had a plan. "Tommorrow there's a hunt. If we all go, we could slip away together." Everyone agreed.

The next day the Time trekkers accompanied Lady Eleanor and her falcons. As dusk fell, they crept behind a bush and watched as the hunt galloped off into the distance. On the other side of the hedge, men and children were still hard at work in the fields. When they finally headed home, the gang sneaked behind them.

FALCONRY

First, a leash and bells (*right*) are attached to the falcon's foot. Then the owner throws scraps of food into the air for the falcon to catch. Eventually, the falcon flies free, killing small birds and taking them to the owner. When at rest, it wears a hood over its eyes (*left*). Lady Eleanor wears a glove (*top*) to protect her arm from its claws.

How do they train a falcon to do that?
Why are the fields in strips?

STRIP FARMING

Each village has three large fields which are divided into small strips. The villagers farm some strips in each field, so that the good and bad land is equally divided.

Peasants depend on crops as they are not allowed to hunt or fish. Each year they agree on what to sow in each field: grass for the animals; wheat for bread; or barley for beer.

Oxen are used for plowing and heavy loads, but the rest of the work is done by hand (*right*).

Why's he been put in there?

PUNISHMENT

All criminals are punished in public. The pickpocket will be locked in the stocks for two days and mocked by the rest of the villagers. He is lucky not to be hanged.

If he had been found stealing valuables or livestock he would have faced death. Nobles are beheaded rather than hanged, though many pay to be let free. Executions also take place in public, and large crowds turn out to watch (*below*).

Ahead of them, on the road, a young girl struggled with a huge load of straw. Jools offered to give her a hand. Her name was Rebecca. She was only 10 years old, but she had been at work since sunrise that morning.

As they entered the village they heard shouting coming from the green. A boy was locked up in the stocks and a crowd had gathered to throw rotten fruit and jeer. Suddenly, Sam yelled for joy. "Look what's around his neck," she cried, "It's the time machine key!" So ducking the flying fruit, she ran up and grabbed it.

CHILDHOOD

Children in the Middle Ages don't go to school. Instead, they are taught the skills they will need in adult life by their parents.

In peasant families this means helping in the fields. The youngest children have to scare the birds from newly sown corn (*above*).

Girls also help with household chores and learn to spin and cook. Boys help out with heavier work (*right*).

When Rebecca realized the Time trekkers had nowhere to go, she insisted they come to her family's house. It was very different from the castle. Her entire family lived in one room, which was smokey, damp, and cold, and part of the same room was divided into stalls for the animals.

All eyes were on Rebecca's mom who was stirring a large pot over the fire. Just as she started to serve the meal, there was a crash at the door. It was Baron John's soldiers. They had come for the Time trekkers.

DAILY ROUTINE

No wonder she's tired. She has to nurse the baby, light the fire (*left*), feed the animals, wake the children, roll up the mattress, sweep the floor, make breakfast, fetch water from the well, work in the garden, fetch firewood, milk the cow (*above*), collect the eggs, spin the wool, make supper, put the children to bed, mend their clothes, (*left*) and finally... fall asleep!

Your mom looks tired.
Mmm. What's for dinner?
A PEASANT'S FOOD
Unlike Baron John, Rebecca's family eat a very simple diet based on vegetables (*above*). Tonight, it's "pottage," a thick pea soup, served with dark brown bread. There might be a scrap of meat in it, if you're very lucky.
Most families only have one pot, so all dishes are cooked together. That's if there is anything to eat. Famine is a constant threat.
T

How can they accuse us of witchcraft?
WITCHCRAFT
Medieval people are suspicious of anyone different and, let's face it, you four must seem quite strange. You also disobeyed Baron John, and ran away from the monastery.
But the final straw was probably when they found the time machine. That convinced them all that you are witches, because in a world without electricity and cars, even Sam's Walkman would seem to work by magic.
T

The gang tried to hide but the soldiers soon found them. They were marched back to the castle, put in chains, and flung into a cold, dark dungeon.

"What's going on?" moaned Jools the next morning. "Oh no," shrieked Sam, who had scrambled up onto Lucy's shoulders to peek through the tiny window. "I think they're going to burn us at the stake. They've found the time machine and they must think we're witches." Eddie started to tremble. "Wait a minute," cried Sam, "there seems to be some trouble. In fact, I think the castle is under attack!"

I think I'm catching a cold.

MEDICINE

Don't tell the doctors! They think all illness is caused by "bad" blood. They'll cut open your vein and let you bleed for awhile or use leeches (wormlike creatures that suck out your blood). Surgery is even worse. There are no painkillers or antiseptic, so patients often die of infection. Herbal remedies are also used and are probably quite effective (*right*).

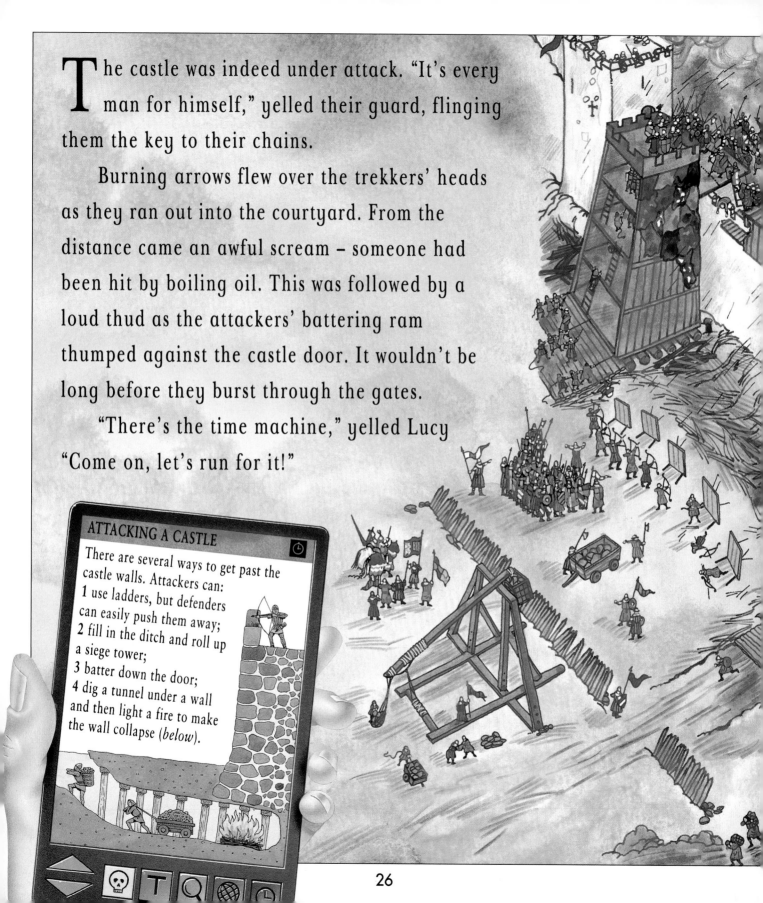

The castle was indeed under attack. "It's every man for himself," yelled their guard, flinging them the key to their chains.

Burning arrows flew over the trekkers' heads as they ran out into the courtyard. From the distance came an awful scream – someone had been hit by boiling oil. This was followed by a loud thud as the attackers' battering ram thumped against the castle door. It wouldn't be long before they burst through the gates.

"There's the time machine," yelled Lucy "Come on, let's run for it!"

ATTACKING A CASTLE

There are several ways to get past the castle walls. Attackers can:
1 use ladders, but defenders can easily push them away;
2 fill in the ditch and roll up a siege tower;
3 batter down the door;
4 dig a tunnel under a wall and then light a fire to make the wall collapse (*below*).

DEFENDING A CASTLE

The defenders have built wooden galleries that overhang the walls.

From these they can throw rocks (*below*) or boiling oil (*right*) onto the attackers as they try to climb up.

They also fire arrows through special narrow slits in the wall. But the most important thing is to stock up on supplies – many castles surrender because the defenders run out of food.

Eddie wiggled a few knobs and transported them forward 300 years. "I just want to see how the Middle Ages end," he explained. They landed in a large square, surrounded by ornate buildings. "We're in Venice," shouted Lucy, who recognized St. Mark's Square from a travel guide she had at home.

EXPLORATION
They have come from eastern countries of China and India, probably inspired by Marco Polo, an Italian who traveled to China. He kept a diary of his adventures and brought back many exotic goods.
So far, no one has gone west. In 1492 Christopher Colombus will set sail, hoping to find a new route to the East. Instead, he'll be the first European to see America.
Where have they been?

Elegantly dressed men and women strolled through the piazza, stopping to admire the exotic foreign goods on display at several stalls. Two gentlemen were discussing the shape of the Earth – was it flat or round? They seemed surprised when Sam assured them it was round!

THE RENAISSANCE

The Renaissance has happened! Renaissance means "rebirth" and it refers to this period (the 15th century) when lots of new ideas are being explored. There are new inventions; new styles of painting and architecture; new scientific experiments, and new ideas about politics and religion. One of the most famous inventors is Leonardo da Vinci who sketches all kinds of inventions, such as an early parachute (*above*).

Jools was hungry, and although the Renaissance seemed a lot better than what had come before, he had seen enough of Middle Age hygiene to never want to eat again. "Let's go," he said, "We should be just in time for supper." He pressed the PRESENT button and the machine burst into action.

As his stomach rumbled loudly, he thought back to the meager meal they had shared with Rebecca and her family, and the lavish feast they had served to Baron John and his guests.

"Life in the Middle Ages seems so unequal," he said.

"Yeah, and violent," added Eddie, who was still quaking at the thought of being burned at the stake. "Well," said Lucy, "at least we got to see a castle – and even the dungeons!"

THE GIZMO PUZZLER

1. Baron John lives in a castle. What other types of buildings can you spot?
2. How do medieval people travel?
3. What animals do they keep?
4. The Time trekkers are accused of witchcraft because of the time machine. However, medieval people used various devices to make their life easier. Can you find them all?
5. The pickpocket appears on pages 7, 9, 15, 16, and 20. But where is he?
6. Can you spot Jools' frog, Kevin?

The Answers — Just turn the book upside down and look at it in a mirror!

1. Wooden fort (page 5); town houses, church (8–9); stables (13); monastery, cathedral, garden shed; (14–15); bakery and town houses (16–17); church, windmill, smithy, tavern (20–21); cottage (22–23); dungeon (24–25), church, city buildings (28–29).
2. Riding (4–5, 6–7, 8–9, 12–13, 18, 19); ships and boats (6, 28); carts (7, 12, 15); on a chair (7, on the bridge); on stilts (9) and walking!
3. Pigs (4–5, 16, 22), sheep (4–5), oxen (6, 19, 21), dogs (6, 10, 12), bear (9), bees (15), cows (15, 17), cats (17), falcons (16–17), chickens (17, 21, 23).
4. Ovens to bake bread (12); forges to make iron (13, 20); machines to practice jousting (13); grinder to sharpen swords (13); winch to lift blocks of stone (14); plough (19); windmill to grind corn (20); well (21); siege machine (26); battering ram (27).
5. Next to ox cart (7); behind Sam (9); behind ox cart (15); behind Lucy (16); in stocks (20).
6. In Jools' pocket (5); on Jools' shoulder (9); on bowl near musicians (11); on Jools' shoulder (21); on bench (23); on skull (25); in lady's hat above Jools (29); on the time machine (30).

A Quick History of The Middle Ages

476 A.D. The end of the Roman Empire in Europe, and the end of the ancient world.

400–800 During this period most of Europe is converted to Christianity.

500–800 The Dark Ages, a time of constant wars, and a decline in town life and trade.

800 Charlemagne unites most of western Europe, and is crowned Holy Roman Emperor.

800–900 The start of the feudal system (in which the king gives land to his barons in return for their support).

1066 William of Normandy invades England.

1080s The first stone castles are built in Europe (*above*).

1096 Pope Urban launches the First Crusade to recapture Jerusalem from the Muslims (*above*).

1100–1200 The Church becomes the single great force, bringing the small states of Europe together.

The Pope is as powerful as any king, and great cathedrals are built all over Europe.

1215 The signing of the Magna Carta reduces the power of the King of England over the barons.

1300–1500 Medieval Europe is slowly transformed as the Renaissance leads to many scientific discoveries, new styles of art, and religious ideas.

1337–1453 The Hundred Years' War between France and England begins an era of civil war and rebellion throughout Europe.

1347–1351 The Black Death kills 25 million people across Europe (*left*).

1453 Constantinople is captured by the Turks, marking the end of the Middle Ages.

1492 Christopher Columbus sails to the Americas (*above*).

Index

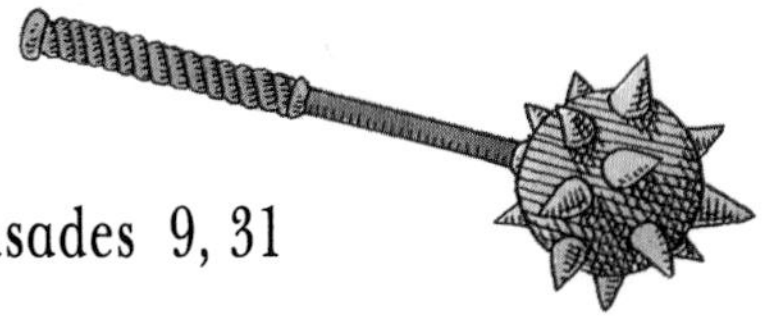

	DATE DUE		